# Future Energy

by Helen Orme

By Helen Orme

Series consultant: Terry Jennings

*ticktock* editor: Sophie Furse

*ticktock* designer: Hayley Terry

Picture research: Lizzie Knowles

With thanks to: Mark Sachner, Joe Harris and Claire Lucas

Copyright © ticktock Entertainment Ltd 2008

First published in Great Britain in 2008 by ticktock Media Ltd,
Unit 2, Orchard Business Centre, North Farm Road,
Tunbridge Wells, Kent, TN2 3XF

ISBN 978 1 84696 738 2 pbk
Printed in China

A CIP catalogue record for this book is available from the British Library.

Picture credits
Age fotostock/SuperStock: 18-19. Martin Bond/ Science Photo Library: 13c, 27b. Prof. David Hall/ Science Photo Library: 27t.
Mehau Kulyk/ Science Photo Library: 20. Chiara Levi/ iStock: 29b. Ria Novosti/ Science Photo Library 17t. Norman
Pogson/iStock: OBC. Shutterstock: OFC, 1, 2, 4, 5, 6t, 6-7, 7t, 8, 9 all, 10-11, 11c, 12-13, 14, 15, 16-17, 22, 22-23, 24, 25t,
25b, 26r, 28t, 28b, 29t, 29c, 30, 31, 32. Pasquale Sorrentino/ Science Photo Library 21. ticktock Media Archive: 23, 26l.
Every effort has been made to trace the copyright holders, and we apologise in advance for any unintentional omissions.
We would be pleased to insert the appropriate acknowledgements in any subsequent edition of this publication.

# CONTENTS

Words that appear **in bold** are explained in the glossary.

# THE ENERGY PROBLEM

*People can't live without energy. We need it for food, heat and light, and to travel from one place to another. We also need it to power our homes and businesses.*

Most of the energy we use comes from fuels such as coal, oil and gas. Using these fuels has begun to cause problems. One problem is that supplies of some of these fuels are running out.

*Oil rigs drill for fuel deep underground.*
*Some stand on stilts in the ocean.*

Another problem is that the way we use energy from these fuels creates **pollution**, which is harmful to the **environment**. Scientists are finding new ways to make energy that will not harm the environment.

# NON-RENEWABLE ENERGY

Most of the energy we use is made from **non-renewable** resources, such as oil, gas, and coal. They are being used up faster than they can be replaced.

*Burning gas.*

Oil, gas, and coal are **fossil fuels**. When fossil fuels are burned, they give off gases, such as carbon dioxide, that pollute the environment.

*A coal-burning power station.*

If there is too much carbon dioxide in the **atmosphere**, heat from the Sun cannot easily escape back into space after reaching the Earth. This will make Earth warmer and change weather patterns. This could seriously affect all life on Earth. We need to find other ways to make energy.

*Burning coal.*

# RENEWABLE ENERGY

*Some types of energy are produced from renewable resources. This kind of energy will not run out or get less over time.*

Types of renewable energy are solar, movement of the wind, the **tides** of the sea, nuclear power, and the force of water rushing down a hill.

The energy from burning wood and plants is also a renewable resource, if we plant new trees to replace what we cut down.

If we use these sources instead of fossil fuels, we will be able to produce enough energy in ways that don't damage the planet.

*In the future, we may find a reliable way of capturing the renewable energy of ocean waves.*

# WHAT IS CLEAN ENERGY?

'Clean' energy does not produce polluting gases, such as carbon dioxide, or produces only small amounts of them. One way to make clean energy is to change how we burn fossil fuels. We need to find ways to burn these fuels that do not give off lots of gas.

*This machine uses solar energy to heat water.*

An even better way to produce clean energy is to burn less fossil fuels. We can use renewable energy sources such as the Sun, wind, and waves instead. These make clean energy.

## POWER FROM WATER

The force of river water pouring through a dam can make lots of clean electricity. However, large dams can harm the **habitats** of thousands of plants and animals.

# WIND AND WAVE POWER

Wind turbines produce clean, renewable energy. The energy in the wind turns the windmill-like blades on the turbine. These blades are connected to a **rotor**. This spins a **generator**, which creates electricity.

Wind turbines standing in the ocean.

There are, however, a few problems with using wind power. **Wind turbines** only produce energy when the wind blows. They are also huge and can force wildlife off the land they are built on. One answer to this problem is to build the turbines at sea or on large lakes.

Waves and tides are also good sources of clean energy. Why? They never stop coming and going!

*Some tidal power stations trap incoming water inside dams. When the tide goes out, the water is released. The fast-flowing water is used to produce energy.*

# ENERGY FOR LIFE - THE SUN

*The Sun is Earth's biggest energy source. Today there are ways to turn sunlight directly into energy we need. One way is by using **solar panels**.*

Some solar panels trap sunlight to make electricity. These are made up of solar cells. The cells change the energy in sunlight into electrical power. This is a great way to get clean energy. Another kind of solar panel heats up water. However, solar panels don't work at night!

In the future, it may be possible to put big solar panels into space and send the power down to Earth. The Sun always shines in space!

## STORING ENERGY

Finding new ways to store energy is as important as finding new ways to produce it. Knowing how to store solar energy would mean we could even use solar power at night.

*Solar power stations trap sunlight to bring power to homes and businesses.*

# NUCLEAR POWER

*Nuclear power stations use nuclear energy to produce electricity. Nuclear energy is released from chemicals like* **uranium***. This process uses a lot of water, but it doesn't make any carbon dioxide or other harmful gases.*

However, there are problems with nuclear power. The stations are expensive to build and run. They also produce small amounts of dangerous waste that can sicken or kill living things. Nuclear waste must be kept safe for thousands of years. Scientists are working on new types of nuclear power that may solve some of these problems.

Uranium is mined from deep underground. There may not be enough uranium in the world to keep stations like the one shown here working in the future.

# CLEANING UP COAL

Our planet's coal supplies will last longer than oil.
However coal is a non-renewable energy source
because it takes so long for more of it to form.
Burning coal gives off more polluting gases than
any other fossil fuel.

There are cleaner ways that coal can be used. One way is to wash the coal with chemicals before it is burnt, or spray the polluting gases with special chemicals to clean them.

Another way is to store the polluting gases from burning coal deep underground, or in containers in the sea. However, some scientists feel that these methods may also harm the environment.

*A coal-burning power station in Westphalia, Germany.*

*A one-seater electric car
at a charging point.*

# ELECTRIC AND HYBRID CARS

*Fuel for cars, buses and trucks mainly comes from oil. Our supply of oil will not last forever, however. Burning oil also creates pollution.*

Electric cars do not produce harmful gases. They would make cities much cleaner places. These cars run from electricity stored in batteries. If the electricity comes from power stations that use fossil fuels, these cars may not be the best way to reduce the use of fossil fuels.

Hybrid cars are powered by both oil and electricity. A hybrid car can store electricity while it runs on fuel. Then, when it is stopped, braking, or going downhill, it can switch to electric power and save fuel.

## FUEL CELLS – ANOTHER ALTERNATIVE POWER SOURCE?

Fuel cells like the ones shown here combine hydrogen and oxygen to generate electrical power. They may be an important source of energy for fuelling cars and even homes in the future.

# BIOMASS ENERGY

*Fossil fuel supplies are running out, especially oil. One solution is to use renewable energy sources that produce fuels from **biomass**.*

Biomass includes plants such as corn, trees and sugar cane (below). Biomass also includes waste from plants, such as sawdust, grass clippings or peanut shells.

Burning biomass does release carbon dioxide. But if this release can be balanced by a way of removing carbon dioxide, such as planting trees, then the biomass is said to be **carbon neutral**.

Many scientists feel that biomass is the best source of energy for the future. However other scientists argue that if biomass is used for fuel instead of food, people in some parts of the world will not have enough to eat.

**Sugar cane**

# CARBON-NEUTRAL ENERGY FROM WOOD

Burning wood releases carbon dioxide into the atmosphere. However, new trees will take carbon dioxide out of the atmosphere. By planting new trees, we can ensure that wood is a carbon-neutral energy source.

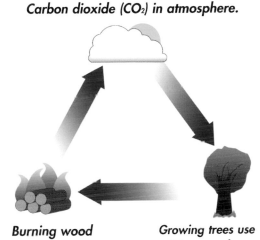

Carbon dioxide ($CO_2$) in atmosphere.

Burning wood releases $CO_2$ back into atmosphere.

Growing trees use $CO_2$ to produce their food.

*Corn is harvested on a farm in the Midwest of the USA. The corn can be used to create biomass energy.*

23

## SAVING ENERGY

*The best way to save energy, and help the environment, is to use less of it. Houses of the future will be built to save energy and could even produce their own energy. However, there are ways people can start saving energy today.*

**Top tips to save energy:**

• Wear more layers of clothes so you can turn down the heating.

• Don't dry your clothes in the tumble dryer.

• Close your curtains or blinds at night to keep the heat in.

• Switch off the lights when you leave a room.

• When you've finished watching TV or using the computer, turn them off.

• Use low-energy light bulbs.

• Re-use or recycle materials.

Hanging your clothes out to dry instead of using a tumble dryer will save lots of energy.

## CARS, LORRIES AND GREENHOUSE GASES

*People everywhere drive cars. In the UK, there are*
*375 cars for every 1,000 people.*

• Most cars are fuelled by petrol, which is a fossil fuel. Burning fossil fuels creates **greenhouse gases**. These gases help keep Earth warm. However, making too much of these greenhouse gases could lead to the melting of ice at the North and South Poles. It could also cause other dangerous changes to the environment.

**Walking to school with your friends is a great way to save energy.**

• One way to reduce greenhouse gases is to use cars less. Try walking, cycling, or using public transport. If you have school friends that live near you, why not suggest walking together to make it more fun.

• A large number of lorries are carrying food grown in other countries. Eating locally grown food could decrease the number of lorries on the road.

• Over a quarter of the lorries on the road are empty. They are travelling back after delivering their cargo. If they collected another cargo for their return trip, then they could be more **energy efficient**.

# FUTURE TRANSPORT – PLANES VS. TRAINS

*Worldwide, about 81,000 planes take off each day. In 2003, 200 million people travelled by plane. By 2030, this number may double to 400 million. More and more people are travelling by plane – and this means more and more greenhouses gases.*

**18.3kg**

**14.7 kg**

**5.2 kg**

*Kilograms of carbon dioxide*

**Planes    Cars    Trains**

• This chart (left) shows how much carbon dioxide is produced by 100 passengers travelling 100 kilometres. As you can see, trains create less carbon dioxide than either cars or planes, and are therefore less harmful to the environment.

• How can we make a difference? We could try to use planes less often. For short trips, we could travel by train. We could plan holidays in our own country, or in countries we can reach by train.

# FACTFILE

## CASE STUDY – BIOGAS PLANTS IN INDIA

*In Indian villages, burning wood is an important way to cook food. However, there isn't enough wood for everyone. To solve this problem, many houses in India have **biogas** plants outside.*
*Biogas is produced by waste that has been decaying, or rotting for a while.*

A biogas plant outside a home in India.

• How does a biogas plant work? First, people put household waste and food scraps into a tank. Then, as the waste rots, **methane** gas is produced. This gas can be used as a fuel for cooking, just as natural gas is used in many homes in the UK.

• On a bigger scale, the gas from biogas plants can also be used as fuel in power stations that produce electricity.

A large-scale biogas plant.

## DO WE REALLY NEED HUGE POWER STATIONS?

*Big power stations like the one shown here make huge amounts of electricity. It's not enough, however, to just produce electricity.*

**A coal power station.**

• The electricity must then be sent to where it's needed. To do this, power companies build long cables and huge towers, or pylons, like those shown below, to support those cables. We need pylons to carry electricity from the station into our homes and businesses. However, many people think they are ugly. They also disturb many types of wildlife on land and in the air.

• New technology means it is now possible to produce electricity for a few houses, or even just one house.

Small power plants can use a variety of ways to produce electricity. Many of these, as shown in the next Factfile, can be from renewable energy sources.

**Pylons carry electricity cables above ground.**

## MAKING YOUR OWN ELECTRICITY

*Future homes will be more energy efficient. Some may even make their own electricity. Here are some ways that homes may make their own electricity – perhaps even enough to share with other homes:*

Small wind turbines.

• Small wind turbines can make electricity whenever a breeze is blowing.

• More homes in the future will have solar panels on their roofs. Although they are most effective when the Sun is shining directly on them, they will also make power when it's cloudy, rainy, or snowy.

• Scientists are working on ways to store solar energy so buildings can also be powered at night.

Solar panels provide energy.

Fuel cells can generate power.

• In the future, more homes may be equipped with fuel cells, as shown on the left. Fuel cells contain hydrogen and oxygen, which when combined will generate electrical power. These cells may replace boilers as a way to heat water.

29

# WHAT YOU CAN DO

### Here are some action tips
### for becoming an energy saver:

• Persuade your school to do a project
on saving energy. Ask your teacher
how you can find out how much
electricity your school uses. Then
set a target for how much you
can save every week. Keep a
record of your school's usage and
see how it changes from week to week.

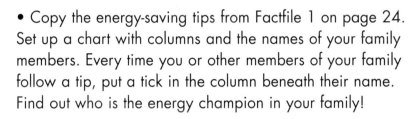

• Copy the energy-saving tips from Factfile 1 on page 24.
Set up a chart with columns and the names of your family
members. Every time you or other members of your family
follow a tip, put a tick in the column beneath their name.
Find out who is the energy champion in your family!

• Organise a 'walk to school' week. If it's too far to walk, try
cycling instead. You never know — your family might enjoy it
so much that you will want to do it all the time!

### Visit these websites for more
### information and to find out how you
### can help save energy.

The Atmosphere, Climate and Environment Information Programme:
www.ace.mmu.ac.uk/kids

Energy Saving Trust: www.energysavingtrust.org.uk

California Energy Commission: www.energyquest.ca.gov

# GLOSSARY

**atmosphere** The thick layer of air that surrounds the Earth.

**biomass** Plants or parts of plants – such as stems and leaves – that can be used as fuels, or to make fuels.

**biogas** Gas from waste that can be used as fuel.

**carbon neutral** A process that takes the same amount of carbon dioxide out of the atmosphere as it produces.

**energy efficient** Designed to use up as few natural resources as possible to make energy and to prevent energy loss.

**environment** An area or place where people, plants, and animals live.

**fossil fuels** Fuels such as gas, oil and coal made from living things that died millions of years ago.

**generator** A machine that produces electricity.

**greenhouse gases** Gases that help warm the planet by preventing heat from escaping from the atmosphere into space.

**habitats** Areas where plants or animals are usually found. Most habitats are suited to certain kinds of life, such as fish (in a water habitat).

**methane** A natural gas that can be made from rotting waste and used for energy.

**mined** Removed from deep in the Earth.

**non-renewable** Produced from resources that will eventually run out, like coal or oil.

**pollution** Unwanted chemicals and other substances that harm the air, water, or land.

**renewable** Produced from resources that will not run out, such as wind, water, or sunlight.

**rotor** A part, like a propeller or windmill blade, that rotates around a central, fixed point in a machine.

**solar panels** A device that traps energy from the Sun and changes it into electrical power.

**tides** The natural rising and falling of the sea level every day.

**uranium** A metal found deep underground that can be used in producing nuclear energy.

**wind turbines** Machines that turn the power of the wind into electricity.

# INDEX